Giving Than

The Pilgrims sailed to America.
They were thankful for their new home.

2

I am thankful for my new home.

The Pilgrims came to America to be free.
They were thankful for their freedom.

I am thankful for my freedom.

The Pilgrims wanted to learn about the world.
They were thankful for their schools.

I am thankful for my school.

The Pilgrims met new people in America.
They were thankful for their new friends.

I am thankful for my new friends.

The Pilgrims had a hard winter.
They were thankful for people who helped them.

I am thankful for people who help me.

The Pilgrims' families worked together.
They were thankful for their families.

I am thankful for my family.

On the first Thanksgiving,
the Pilgrims were thankful for their feast.

This Thanksgiving, I am thankful for my feast.

And I am thankful for the Pilgrims.